W9-BAT-453

DATE DUE			SEP 17
AUG 1 0 '99			
FEB 2 6 2002			

J
599.725   Wexo, John
WEX   Bonnett
             Wild horses

 Bound to Stay Bound Books, Inc.

WILD HORSES

Published by Creative Education, 123 South Broad Street, Mankato, Minnesota 56001

Copyright © 1996 by Wildlife Education, Ltd. Copyright 1996 hardbound edition by Creative Education. All rights reserved. No part of this book may be reproduced in any form without written permission from the publisher. Printed in the United States.

Printed by permission of Wildlife Education, Ltd.

Library of Congress Cataloging-in-Publication Data

Wexo, John Bonnett.
Wild horses / created and written by John Bonnett Wexo: zoological consultant,
Charles R. Schroeder: scientific consultants, James Dolan, Oliver A. Ryder, David P.
Willoughby.
p. cm. — (Zoobooks)
Includes index.
Summary: Examines the physical characteristics, habits, and natural environment of
various species of wild horses, now foiund only in Africa, Asia—and in zoos.
ISBN 0-88682-781-7
1. Wild horses—Juvenile literature. [1. Wild horses.] I. Title. II. Series: Zoo books
(Mankato, Minn.)
SF360.W48   1996
599.72'5-dc20   95-45322   CIP AC

WILD HORSES

MARTIN COUNTY LIBRARY SYSTEM
701 EAST OCEAN BLVD.
STUART, FLORIDA 34994-2374

Creative Education

Art Credits

Pages Six and Seven: Barbara Hoopes

Pages Eight and Nine: Barbara Hoopes

Pages Ten and Eleven: Mark Hallett

Page Twelve: Ed Zilberts; **Upper Right,** Walter Stuart

Page Thirteen: Ed Zilberts; **Upper Right,** Walter Stuart and Ed Zilberts

Page Sixteen: Barbara Hoopes; **Lower Right,** John Roy

Page Seventeen: Barbara Hoopes; **Far Right,** Walter Stuart

Page Eighteen: Barbara Hoopes; **Upper Left,** Karl Edwards

Page Nineteen: Barbara Hoopes; **Upper Right,** Karl Edwards

Page Twenty: Walter Stuart

Page Twenty-One: Top, Karl Edwards; **Middle Right,** Pamela Stuart

Photographic Credits

Front Cover: Peter Pickford (DRK Photo)

Page Thirteen: Aldo Margiocco

Pages Fourteen and Fifteen: Gregory G. Dimijian, M.D. (*Photo Researchers*)

Page Sixteen: Henry Ausloos (*Animals Animals*)

Page Nineteen: Upper Right, Tom McHugh (*Photo Researchers*); **Center,** Gail Rubin (*Photo Researchers*)

Page Twenty: Lower Right, Courtesy of the British Museum

Page Twenty-One: Middle Left, (*Musée de St. Germain*); **Lower Right,** Lee Boltin

Pages Twenty-Two and Twenty-Three: Erwin and Peggy Bauer (*Bruce Coleman, Inc.*)

Our Thanks To: Mary Littauer; Ayako Imai Jim Pfeiffer and Dr. Karl Frucht (*World Society of the Protection of Animals*); Lynnette Wexo.

Contents

Wild horses ———————————— 6-7

Wild horses are built for speed ————— 8-9

More than 250 types of horses ———— 10-11

Zebras ———————————— 12-13

Mongolian wild horses ————— 16-17

Wild asses ———————————— 18-19

People and horses ————————— 20-21

The future of wild horses ———————— 22-23

Index ———————————— 24

Wild horses are found today only in Africa and Asia—and in zoos, of course. Only zebras, wild asses, and Mongolian wild horses are *true* wild horses. All other horses and donkeys are called domestic (doe-MESS-tick) horses. They are different from wild horses because people have changed their anatomy and behavior over the years by selective breeding and training. Domestic horses that escape or are set free into the wild are called feral (FER-ul) horses. They are not really wild horses.

All horses, domestic and wild, are related closely enough to be included in a single general scientific category—the genus *Equus* (GEE-nus EE-kwis). Very young horses are called foals (FOE-lz). Adult males are known as stallions (STAL-yunz), while adult females are called mares (MAIR-z).

GREVY'S ZEBRA
Equus grevyi

DAMARALAND ZEBRA
Equus burchelli antiquorum

SOMALI WILD ASS
Equus africanus somalicus

Mongolian Wild Horses
Equus caballus przewalskii

Kiang
Equus hemionus kiang

Nubian Wild Ass
Equus africanus africanus

Cape Mountain Zebra
Equus zebra zebra

7

Wild horses are built for speed.

This is because speed is the best way for a horse to stay alive. On the open plains, where most wild horses live, there are few places to hide from predators. So horses must outrun attackers, taking big strides with their long legs. They have strong muscles and large lungs, and this gives them the ability to keep running fast for a long time — for hours, if necessary. A running horse is not only beautiful, but *safe*.

At first glance, a zebra or a wild ass may look very different from the Mongolian wild horse shown below. But the differences are only skin deep. The color and pattern of the coat may be different. Or the length of the mane. Or the shape of the ears and tail. But underneath these surface things, all wild horses are very much the same. In fact, horse experts sometimes have a hard time telling the skeleton of a zebra from the skeleton of a Mongolian wild horse.

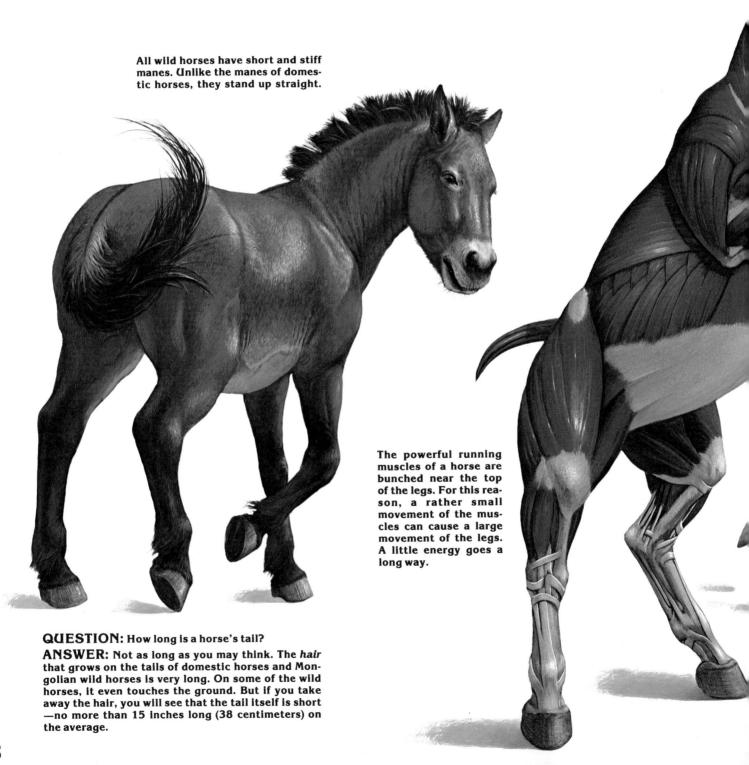

All wild horses have short and stiff manes. Unlike the manes of domestic horses, they stand up straight.

The powerful running muscles of a horse are bunched near the top of the legs. For this reason, a rather small movement of the muscles can cause a large movement of the legs. A little energy goes a long way.

QUESTION: How long is a horse's tail?
ANSWER: Not as long as you may think. The *hair* that grows on the tails of domestic horses and Mongolian wild horses is very long. On some of the wild horses, it even touches the ground. But if you take away the hair, you will see that the tail itself is short —no more than 15 inches long (38 centimeters) on the average.

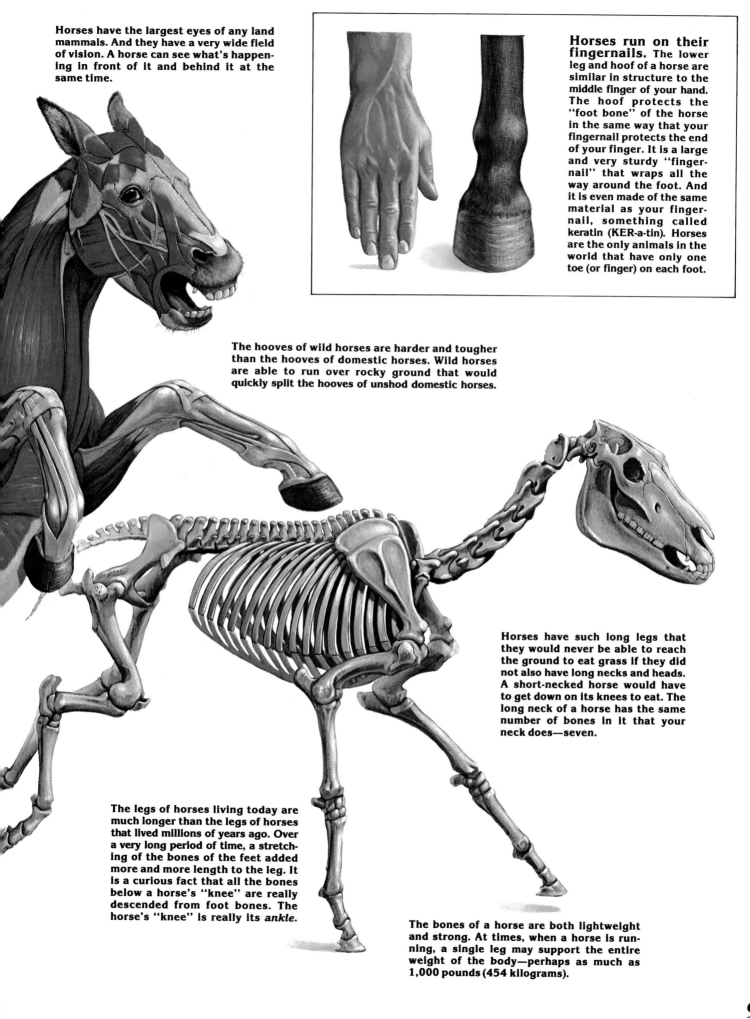

Horses have the largest eyes of any land mammals. And they have a very wide field of vision. A horse can see what's happening in front of it and behind it at the same time.

Horses run on their fingernails. The lower leg and hoof of a horse are similar in structure to the middle finger of your hand. The hoof protects the "foot bone" of the horse in the same way that your fingernail protects the end of your finger. It is a large and very sturdy "fingernail" that wraps all the way around the foot. And it is even made of the same material as your fingernail, something called keratin (KER-a-tin). Horses are the only animals in the world that have only one toe (or finger) on each foot.

The hooves of wild horses are harder and tougher than the hooves of domestic horses. Wild horses are able to run over rocky ground that would quickly split the hooves of unshod domestic horses.

Horses have such long legs that they would never be able to reach the ground to eat grass if they did not also have long necks and heads. A short-necked horse would have to get down on its knees to eat. The long neck of a horse has the same number of bones in it that your neck does—seven.

The legs of horses living today are much longer than the legs of horses that lived millions of years ago. Over a very long period of time, a stretching of the bones of the feet added more and more length to the leg. It is a curious fact that all the bones below a horse's "knee" are really descended from foot bones. The horse's "knee" is really its *ankle*.

The bones of a horse are both lightweight and strong. At times, when a horse is running, a single leg may support the entire weight of the body—perhaps as much as 1,000 pounds (454 kilograms).

More than 250 different types of horses

have lived on earth since the first horse appeared more than 50 million years ago. The first horse was very small—only about 12 inches high (30 centimeters) at the shoulder. Unlike today's horses, it had four toes on its front feet and three toes on the rear feet. It lived in the forest and ate leaves.

Later horses had longer legs and larger bodies. Over time, the number of toes on the feet was reduced to only one. Many types of horses left the forest and went to live on the plains, where they ate grasses. Scientists tell us that most of the ancestors of today's horses were striped or spotted.

La Brea Tar Pit Quagga
Equus occidentalis

South American Horse
Onohippidium

Forest or Browsing Horse
Hypohippus

Old and New World Grazing Horse
Neohipparion

The First Horse
Hyracotherium

Early Three-toed Horse
Mesohippus

GIANT HORSE
Equus giganteus

AMERICAN ZEBRA
Equus simplicidens

TARPAN
Equus caballus gmelini

QUAGGA
Equus quagga

FIRST GRAZING HORSE
Merychippus

FIRST ONE-TOED HORSE
Pliohippus

MH

11

Zebras seem to be very much alike when you first look at them. But scientists who have studied their behavior and anatomy tell us that there are actually three different types, or species (SPEE-sheez). There are Plains zebras, Mountain zebras, and Grevy's (GREV-eez) zebras.

Plains zebras are the most common zebras. They have very bold stripes, and the stripes on their bodies usually extend down over their stomachs. They live on the open grasslands and along the edges of deserts in East and Central Africa. Usually, 5 to 15 Plains zebras live together in a small family herd. A single stallion leads the family herd, protecting it and keeping it together. Unlike other types of zebras, Plains zebras often eat side by side with other kinds of animals.

Mountain zebras also have bold stripes, but their stomachs are not striped. They have a flap of skin (called a "dewlap") on their necks. They live in mountain areas of southern Africa, in small herds that are similar to Plains zebra herds.

Grevy's zebras are larger than other zebras—often 4 inches (10 centimeters) taller than the average Plains zebra. They have many narrow stripes on their bodies, and their stomachs are not striped. Grevy's zebras do not live in herds.

QUESTION: Are zebras white animals with black stripes, or black animals with white stripes?

ANSWER: Sometimes, zebras are born with stripes that are not fully formed—like the zebra shown above. The patterns on these animals show that the background color of a zebra's coat is probably black. So it seems that zebras are black animals with white stripes.

Like other wild horses, zebras depend on their long legs to carry them to safety when predators approach. When a zebra sees a lion coming, it runs away as fast as it can. As it runs, it zig-zags from side to side, looking back over its shoulder to see if the lion is still chasing it. At other times, a lion may be able to creep up very near to a zebra before it is seen. When a lion charges from so close, the zebra has no time to run. It must fight for its life, biting with its teeth and kicking with its narrow hooves. And the chances are good that the lion will win.

There are probably more than 300,000 Plains zebras in Africa, and the total area in which they are found is very large. Within this total range, there are four regional types (or races) of Plains zebras (one extinct), which have different kinds of stripe patterns. To add to the confusion, there are also two types of Mountain zebras and one type of Grevy's zebra in Africa. Luckily, you can usually tell one type of zebra from another by looking at the stripe pattern on the back end.

Grant's Zebras have very wide and dark stripes on the back end. The legs are striped to the hooves. (A Plains Zebra)

Damaraland Zebras (duh-MAR-a-land) are easily identified by the brownish "shadow stripes" between the black and white stripes on their coats. Usually, the stripes on the legs do not run all the way down to the hooves. (A Plains Zebra)

Grevy's Zebras are not only the largest zebras, but the largest living wild horses as well. They have very large rounded ears, and the leg stripes run all the way down to the hooves.

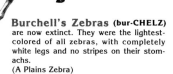

Hartmann's Mountain Zebras are the largest of the Mountain zebras. They look whiter than Cape Mountain zebras because their stripes are more widely spaced.

Selous's Zebras (sell-OO-sez) look a lot like Damaraland zebras, but the "shadow stripes" are usually very faint. Unlike Damaraland zebras, their legs are striped down to the hooves. (A Plains Zebra)

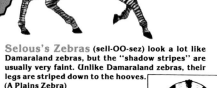

Burchell's Zebras (bur-CHELZ) are now extinct. They were the lightest-colored of all zebras, with completely white legs and no stripes on their stomachs. (A Plains Zebra)

Cape Mountain Zebras are the smallest of all zebras. Like Hartmann's Mountain zebras, they have a string of small stripes above the base of the tail, and "dewlaps" on their necks. Leg stripes run all the way down to the hooves.

Grass is the main food of zebras. They will eat any kind of grass that is available. But their stomachs have a hard time digesting the grass, so zebras must eat a huge amount of it to get the nourishment they need. As a result, they may spend the entire day eating. And in summer, when the days are too hot for eating, they will often feed all night long and rest during the day.

13

Mongolian wild horses are often called Przewalski horses (sheh-VAL-ski) in honor of a Polish explorer who discovered them about a hundred years ago. Of all the wild horses, these animals look the most like domestic horses—and some scientists believe that all domestic horses may be descended from horses of this type.

In general, Mongolian wild horses are smaller than domestic horses, but they have larger heads (and larger brains). Unlike domestic horses, they have a dark stripe running down their backs. There are light-colored rings around both eyes, and the muzzle (or "nose") is also light in color.

Until recently, these beautiful horses lived in mountains and deserts of central Asia—but they have not been seen in the wild since 1968. As you might expect of a desert animal, Mongolian wild horses do not like to go into water, and they can go for several days without drinking. In zoos, they can live as long as many domestic horses—usually 20 to 25 years.

All Mongolian wild horses are brown, but they come in many different shades of brown. Often, very dark horses and very light horses are found in the same herd.

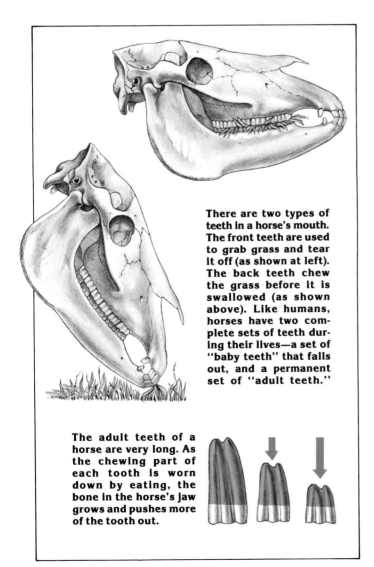

There are two types of teeth in a horse's mouth. The front teeth are used to grab grass and tear it off (as shown at left). The back teeth chew the grass before it is swallowed (as shown above). Like humans, horses have two complete sets of teeth during their lives—a set of "baby teeth" that falls out, and a permanent set of "adult teeth."

The adult teeth of a horse are very long. As the chewing part of each tooth is worn down by eating, the bone in the horse's jaw grows and pushes more of the tooth out.

Within a few hours after it is born, a young wild horse can run fast enough to keep up with the other horses in the herd. It is able to do this because its legs are very long for its size—almost as long as they will be when the horse is fully grown. If baby horses could not run so soon after birth, they would be quickly eaten by predators.

During the winter, the hair of Mongolian wild horses grows longer and thicker. Both males and females grow "beards," and the hair on their necks may get to be 2 or 3 inches long (5 to 8 centimeters). The manes grow longer and may droop over. In spring, this winter coat is shed and replaced by a short summer coat.

Summer Coat

Winter Coat

Unlike domestic horses, Mongolian wild horses shed both their tails and their manes once a year. Domestic horses lose single hairs, which are replaced as they are lost. But Mongolian horses must regrow tails and manes completely every year.

Usually, only one foal is born at a time. The coat of a newborn foal is often very light in color. After 4 or 5 weeks, this is shed and replaced by a darker coat.

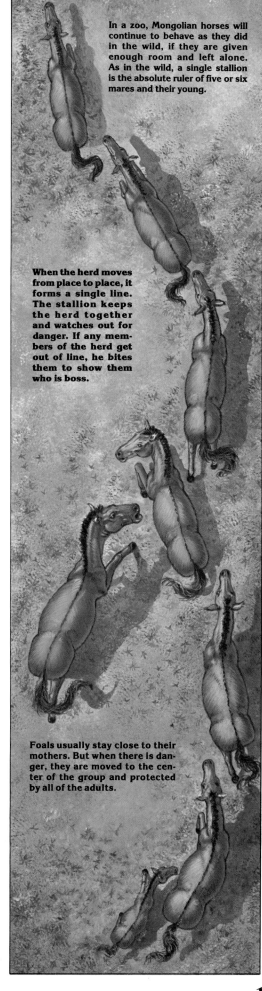

In a zoo, Mongolian horses will continue to behave as they did in the wild, if they are given enough room and left alone. As in the wild, a single stallion is the absolute ruler of five or six mares and their young.

When the herd moves from place to place, it forms a single line. The stallion keeps the herd together and watches out for danger. If any members of the herd get out of line, he bites them to show them who is boss.

Foals usually stay close to their mothers. But when there is danger, they are moved to the center of the group and protected by all of the adults.

17

Wild asses live in some of the most barren places on earth. They seem to thrive in deserts where food and water are often hard to find. They will eat salty grass and drink brackish water that other animals would not touch. And they don't seem to mind temperatures as high as 135 degrees Fahrenheit (57 degrees Celsius)—or as low as 60 degrees below zero Fahrenheit (−51 degrees Celsius).

On the basis of differences in their anatomy and behavior, all wild asses are divided by scientists into two separate groups. Nubian and Somali asses are grouped as African wild asses, and all the others are called Asiatic wild asses.

All wild asses, except kiangs and kulans, spend a lot of time grooming each other. Two animals stand side by side, facing in opposite directions. They gently bite each other's coats. In this way, they are able to clean parts of their bodies that would otherwise be very difficult, or impossible, to reach. Mongolian wild horses and zebras also like to groom.

If you put a kulan into a race with the fastest racehorse of all time—the kulan might win! Even though a kulan is much smaller than a racehorse, it can run at a speed of *more than 40 miles per hour* (64 kilometers per hour).

☐ SOMALI WILD ASSES
▨ NUBIAN WILD ASSES
☐ KULANS
☐ KIANGS
▨ MONGOLIAN WILD ASSES (DZIGETTAI)
■ ONAGERS
▨ INDIAN WILD ASSES (KHUR)

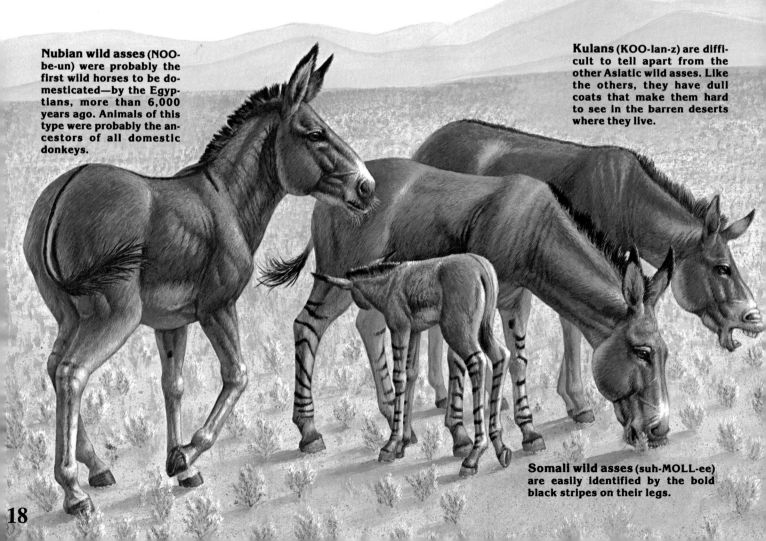

Nubian wild asses (NOO-be-un) were probably the first wild horses to be domesticated—by the Egyptians, more than 6,000 years ago. Animals of this type were probably the ancestors of all domestic donkeys.

Kulans (KOO-lan-z) are difficult to tell apart from the other Asiatic wild asses. Like the others, they have dull coats that make them hard to see in the barren deserts where they live.

Somali wild asses (suh-MOLL-ee) are easily identified by the bold black stripes on their legs.

18

Rolling in dust or mud is a favorite way for all wild horses to get rid of bugs and loose hair. The dust or mud that sticks to them when they stand up also protects them from the heat of the sun and the bites of insects.

The ears of wild asses are much longer than the ears of zebras and Mongolian wild horses. When the young foal below is fully grown, his ears may be more than 8 inches (21 centimeters) long.

All Asiatic wild asses look very much alike and are clearly related to each other. But scientists disagree about the closeness of the relationships. Some say there are three different kinds, or species, and others say there are five.

Herds of wild asses are not led by stallions. An old mare is in charge, and stallions are only seen with the herds during mating season. With kiangs, the leadership of the mare is very strict. The other members of the herd do everything their leader does, as soon as she does it.

When the female leader of a kiang herd starts to run, every member of the herd starts to run. When she turns, they all turn, too.

When the leader stops, the other kiangs stop. When she eats grass, they eat grass. And when she drinks, they all drink. It's really something to see!

Kiangs (KEY-ang-z) are the largest of the wild asses, and the darkest in color. They are also the only wild asses that like to jump into water and swim. All of the other kinds will go to great lengths to avoid even stepping in water.

Onagers (ON-a-jerz) are the smallest of all the wild asses. Like all of the others, they have bulging noses.

19

People and horses have worked together for at least 5,000 years. Before that time, if people wanted to go anywhere, they usually had to walk. If they wanted to take anything with them, they probably had to carry it on their own backs. Then somebody learned how to domesticate (doe-MESS-tick-ate) horses, and all of that was changed.

Domestic horses and donkeys began pulling loads and carrying people on their backs. And because these animals were strong and fast, people found that they could go farther in less time, and carry bigger loads.

In parts of the world where there are no rivers or oceans for boat travel, horses became the best and fastest way to get from place to place. They made it possible for more people to trade with each other, and for armies to move over larger areas. Most of the great civilizations of the past were helped to greatness by the horse.

Within the last 90 years, of course, automobiles have taken the place of horses as the main means of travel on land. But there is no doubt that the history of the world would have been different if wild horses had never existed—or people had never domesticated them.

Oddly enough, the first wild horses trained to pull wagons were probably onagers, the smallest of the wild asses. About 4,600 years ago, the Sumerians (SOO-mare-ee-uns) of ancient Iraq used teams of onagers to pull their war chariots. We know this because a work of art from that time, known as the Standard of Ur, shows a war chariot with four long-eared animals pulling it. A part of this artwork, shown at left, is the basis for the painting above.

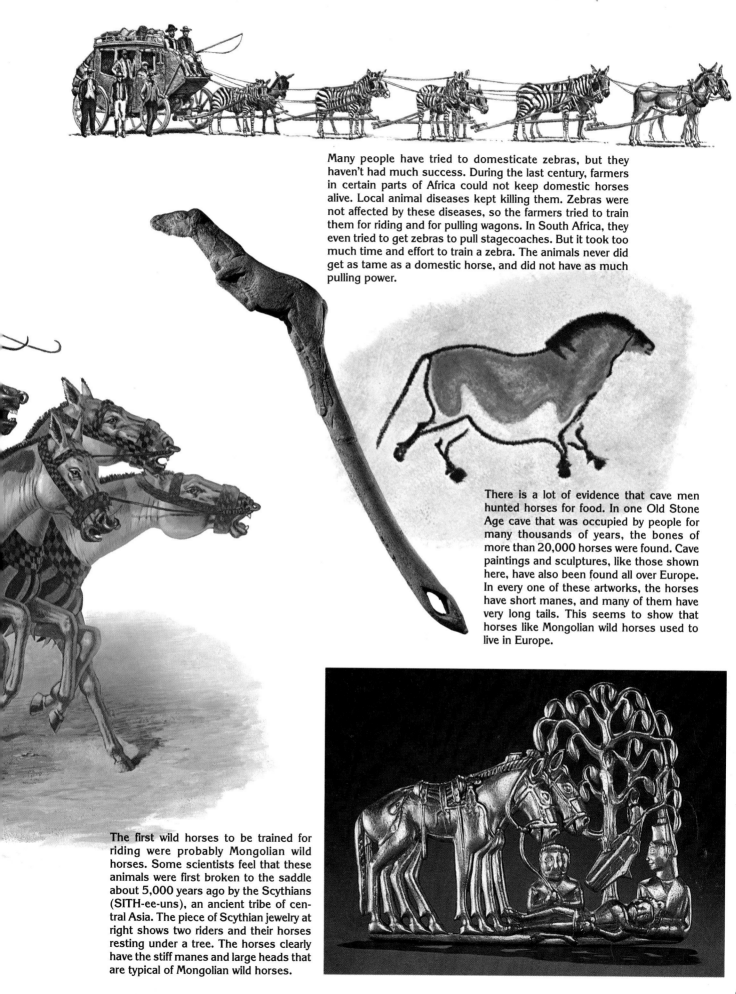

Many people have tried to domesticate zebras, but they haven't had much success. During the last century, farmers in certain parts of Africa could not keep domestic horses alive. Local animal diseases kept killing them. Zebras were not affected by these diseases, so the farmers tried to train them for riding and for pulling wagons. In South Africa, they even tried to get zebras to pull stagecoaches. But it took too much time and effort to train a zebra. The animals never did get as tame as a domestic horse, and did not have as much pulling power.

There is a lot of evidence that cave men hunted horses for food. In one Old Stone Age cave that was occupied by people for many thousands of years, the bones of more than 20,000 horses were found. Cave paintings and sculptures, like those shown here, have also been found all over Europe. In every one of these artworks, the horses have short manes, and many of them have very long tails. This seems to show that horses like Mongolian wild horses used to live in Europe.

The first wild horses to be trained for riding were probably Mongolian wild horses. Some scientists feel that these animals were first broken to the saddle about 5,000 years ago by the Scythians (SITH-ee-uns), an ancient tribe of central Asia. The piece of Scythian jewelry at right shows two riders and their horses resting under a tree. The horses clearly have the stiff manes and large heads that are typical of Mongolian wild horses.

The future of wild horses is up to us. Most of these beautiful animals are now in deep trouble in their natural environments—and some species are among the most endangered animals on earth.

Not long ago, all of the wild horses had much larger ranges than they do now. As recently as 30 years ago, the plains of Africa were still crowded with millions of zebras. Wild asses were still common in many parts of north Africa and Asia. And even Mongolian wild horses seemed to be holding their own in central Asia. But the decline of many of these animals since that time has been rapid and startling.

The number of Hartmann's Mountain zebras has fallen from 50,000 to less than 7,000. There are now fewer than 15,000 Grevy's zebras. Onagers, Kulans, and Somali wild asses have been pushed almost to the vanishing point—there are probably fewer than 500 members of each of these species alive outside of zoos.

It is very possible that Nubian wild asses have vanished entirely from the wild, and there are definitely no more Mongolian wild horses and Cape Mountain zebras running free. These last two species are now found only in zoos, ani-

mal preserves, and national parks.

The reasons for this sad situation are easy to see. Many wild horses lived in areas that people wanted to use for farming and ranching. Some were using water sources that people wanted to use for sheep and other livestock. In order to satisfy their own needs, people simply pushed the wild horses out. They pushed them into some of the most barren and remote areas on earth. And even the horses that could survive in such places, like wild asses, were not safe. People hunted them and hounded them.

Right now, the best hope of most wild horse species lies in the zoos and animal preserves of the world. Already, zoos and preserves have more animals of certain species under protection than remain in the wild. There are, for example, five times as many kulans in captivity as there are in the wild.

If we can keep enough wild horses alive in these protected places, perhaps the time will come when people are a little wiser than they seem to be now. At that future time, maybe the descendants of the wild horses we save today can be released into their natural environment once more, to live as they were meant to live.

Index

African wild asses, 18
Asiatic wild asses, 18-19

Burchell's zebras, 13

Cape mountain zebras, 13,22

Damaraland zebras, 13
Dewlap, 12,13
Domestic horses, 6,9,16,17,20-21
Donkeys, 6,18,20

Ears, 19
Equus, 6
Evolution, of horses, 10-11
Eyes, 9
Eyesight, 9

Feral horses, 6
Foals, 6
    of Mongolian wild horses, 17
    of wild asses, 19

Grant's zebras, 13
Grevy's zebras, 12-13,22
Grooming, 18

Hartmann's mountain zebras, 13,22

Herding
    in Mongolian wild horses, 17
    in wild asses, 19
    in zebras, 12
Hooves, 9
    as defense, 12

Keratin, 9
Kiangs, 18,19
Kulans, 18,22,23

Mane, 8,17
Mares, 6,17,19
Mongolian wild horses, 6,8-9,16-
    17,18,19,21,22
    dominance in, 17
    hair of, 17
    tails of, 17
    young of, 16-17
Mountain zebras, 12-13

Neck, 9
Nubian wild asses, 18,22

Onagers, 18-19,20,22

Plains zebras, 12-13
Przewalski horse
    (see Mongolian wild horse)

Przewalski, 16

Racehorse, 18

Scythians, as domesticators, 21
Selous's zebras, 13
Skeleton, 8-9
Somali wild asses, 18,22
Speed, 8,12,16,18
Stallions, 6,17,19
Stripes, on coats, 10,12-13,16,18
Sumerians, as domesticators, 20
Swimming, by wild asses, 19

Tail, 8,17
Teeth, 16
Transportation, horses as, 20-21

Wild asses, 6,8,18-19,20,22-23
    as prey, 8,12,16,21
    diet of, 18
    distribution of, 18-19

Zebras, 6,8,12-13,18,19,21,22
    diet of, 13
    varieties of, 13
    distribution of, 13
Zigzagging, 12